LITTLE HORSE

For Charlie, without whom so much less.

...so many ways of loving that
all stories should be love stories.

Matt Cohen

We succeed, if we succeed at all
In little sedentary stitches
As if we are making lace.

William Butler Yeats

Contents

LITTLE HORSE

Little Horse   21
Pruning   22
-Aching   23
Room   24
Yellow and Blue   25
My Chest   26
Comedy   27
Between   28
Fine   29
Found   30
Crossing   31
Two   32
This Sisterhood   33
Hard   34
My Breast Still Blooms   35
Halcyon   36
False Pride and the Overpowering Love of Friends   37
Mendelssohn Is Singing   38
Could We Know   39
Love, Come   40
When We Love, Oh, Our Eyes   41
The Grandmother   42
While Talking to My Father   43
Ways   44
Divestiture (Mexico)   45
We Naturally Pray   46

ABUNDANCE

Men Who Play Trombones   49
Holy Week   50
Valentine   51
Turn   52
Singing   53
Medusa (to Perseus)   54
Cwethan: A Legacy   56
What Making Love Is For   57
Pruning (Isobel)   58
Abundance: For Charlie   59
Spring   60
The Entomologist   61
Up   62
Conch   63

ALLUREMENT

Upon My Death: Instructions   67
Allurement: On Reading Jorge Luis Borges'
   This Craft of Verse   68
Seeing Jack Chambers' *Lake Huron #1* Again   69
O – An Essay   70
Allurement (Straychild)   71
Southern Trees   72

Their Beneficence   77
Acknowledgements   79
About the Artist   81
About the Author   83

LITTLE HORSE

LITTLE HORSE
has hitched itself
to the inside
of my skin, slip-
knitted to my nipple;

who would have guessed
its umbilical
genius – it means

to gallop far
and fast
and has tethered itself
to a mothering place.

PRUNING

Last year
our raspberry canes came
fruiting forth four times
the berries of all
other years, a thousand
thousand ruby cells proliferating
into faultless tender
nipples on each
arching wand. In fall
I cut them back.

Last summer and in fall, I bled
from my life a terrible
thronging restlessness that I
keep a secret, but next
Tuesday, when the lab
gets back to me
probably
I'll ask a man who doesn't know
my face
to cut away my breast.

-ACHING
for my daughter
and my sons, as if
they are little
children still, as if
my leaving if
I leave leaves them
lost

and wandering (and me
indignant dying; don't surmise
I am afraid; I'm miles
from that).

ROOM

Over the days, someone might say
my mother is oblivious
to my blunt news, bulletin by bulletin:

> **Mom**
> **a checkup**
> **tests**
> **two labs, tomorrow (Mom!)**

is the cutting day.

Each time she stills herself and I
can feel her absorbing me and maybe gone
as she absorbs still-breathing
absences of mother, father, sisters, brothers
(shattered nature) younger daughter, her
beloved man;
        her stillness
makes an inventory:

still there is room; it can
(again) be done.

YELLOW AND BLUE

In darkness in my cupboard are two
blue-shouldered bottles bought
last year in Maine. They
were full of mountain-water
flown from France, and after I drank
the water, I put away the bottles
for next spring and yellow flowers

… calendulas, I think, although
the thinking makes me lonesome
for my life.

When I die and all's
revealed, my mother and I
will walk together straight
to my mother's dream-cliff and the dusty
rutted road below, where all
along the verges thirty thousand
saffron-yellow flowers bloom;

there they will be – the gypsy
Texas County children 1910, and picking them

>   my mother will say
>   **Imagine such a yellow!**
>   **and the sky blowing around us –**
>   **who could believe such a blue!**

MY CHEST
where my breast
had been
for years
has wept
for seven days

into a tube
to a Hemovac
that saves the tears;

we measure them
in the morning.

COMEDY: I

dis

figure

am

-d.

BETWEEN

I'll set aside some time sometime
go back to 1935 and 565
on Grosvenor Street, to find
the little girl upstairs, who sits
up in the dark and calls
her mother, Say again
what shall I do if we catch fire, jump
out the window (I might break my legs)
or holler help and help, but
everybody on our street's
asleep, or wait for you
and Daddy and the truck with ladders
and a clang and a man climbed up
to save me – will he know?

I'll tell her Sleep
baby, sleep, you lived

and fear between that night and now
is gone, and failure in between
is come undone.

FINE

Thank you for your gift
of soup I am fine
with no breast

and Stargazer lilies I'm
fine
      don't
think of me There
she goes
with no ...
                Charlie
will buy me
an Amazon's dress, a quiver
of arrows, a bow; he

promises me a powerful
aim; he's already fine

with me
with no breast.

FOUND

where my breast was
under the wide gesture
of the scar shaped
like an interrupted
smile, you

can touch the slender
rib bones twelve
years old, and underneath

heart to start
all over again, but
not quite
over again.

CROSSING
alone
is like the thirteenth year
legs slender
tall as a deer
speechless – trusts
murmuring woods
moss
intelligent birds
(fisher, crow)
to be her words
into the next kingdom
its (in spite of everything)
alluring voice.

TWO

Go
to the shadow under the stairs
see
if the child still kicks the wall or
if she's wailed herself to sleep or
if she's humming hastily and tune-
lessly the way she's started to do.
Go
to the false-breast store, buy
two:
one for her bathing suit, the other
manufactured durable
for henceforth every day.

THIS SISTERHOOD

I never meant
to join, I hate
to publicly deny
us (*desaparecidas*, chest
flaps stapled shut) by strapping
on this saddle
with its pocket
with its eerie breast;
                        still

I do it
(in our name
as I might
have dared to not
so do, that also
in our name)
to muffle
the howling absence,
the din.

HARD

It's hard to get to Easter
from this place, me
embracing dirty laundry, and although
I've been to the washing room a dozen
times before, today
I cannot find the stairs, but

wander into a room too vast
for humans; here, large men
and women dressed like Finns before
the War in shiny light-blue suits, their eyes
flat as Little Orphan Annie's,
have come to learn the slow-dance.

A man I know, with an inward smile,
huddles in a crowd of jigsaw
puzzlers, scissoring a puzzle
piece shaped like a 3; he tries
to make it a 6. It's hard

as it's hard (even after
the dream is gone) to
get to Easter; (families

of four and five stroll
eastward, fathers hold the hands
of little sons and daughters, they
adorned as full of light as butterflies:
peach, yellow laundered organdies, short
pants, white shoes as smooth – they
are as smooth as Jordan almonds).

MY BREAST STILL BLOOMS

My gone breast still
strolls synaptic corridors
in my brain, and journeys
to my chest;

a memory-nipple stands
and shimmers there.

HALCYON

A woman that I met
in days unshattered sends
a message from the West, *When next*

we are together, let's
stand side-by-side; we'll
make this tilting star, this
bateau ivre, *symmetrical*
                    (last year
I lost the other-sided breast).

Transfusing notion! Fringe-
capped and poised alert on branches
over the hectic stream (cerulean
dress, our resolute eyes), we fisher-
birds will charm the winds
the waves
to peacefulness.

FALSE PRIDE
AND THE OVERPOWERING LOVE
OF FRIENDS

Their tenderness is a river
bearing her swiftly up; it
has no ears for arms-length
argument, knows
where it's going, dis-
regards her pride as if
it wasn't there at all. It's all

that she can do to keep
her face above the muscle
of the wave.
She goes.

She thinks:
Too fast.
She thinks: Maybe
I'd rather die
than ride this ride.

She thinks about fearless
lovers riding vast and free, giving over
to the river sweeping north
through inundated Carolinian
trees and trees
and tundra, past the darkness
and the bitter wind

to honey
and the Hyperborean sea;
she thinks:
I can imagine that. I remember
ginger flowers.

MENDELSSOHN IS SINGING *How Lovely*
Are the Messengers, I am
swimming naked in a dream I swim
the breast-stroke oh
this pool is Olympic-
size I swim

so long its length and hold
a towel to disguise
the absence of my breast.
                        Astonishing

but I know why these other
swimmers whisper shy
and shocked.
                      I reach

the farther end and, giving up
their eyes, I flip onto my back, I let
the towel float away, I swim
the long, the all the water
back, propel myself with rapid
kicks and sweeping strokes

of my powerful arms and breastless
swim the lengthy all
the water distance
back, my skin

so free; in my under-
water ears I hear
an orchestra.

COULD WE KNOW what
in the world of men's
and women's lives is true, except
that we almost broke before?

Don't be ashamed.
Take pity on us all
for mercy draws courage to it;

this is law
not grace
not even character.

LOVE, COME

play your music like
no other, other
side the ochre road, under
these silver trees. See!
the field is starry blue-
eyed grass. And sand.

      The underhollow
of this shell, it was
an animal, a horseshoe crab
until last year. It lived
like meat, then died; its flesh

unpacked long mortices of cells, col-
lapsed its borders, made
a corridor for air. Come

              play me the way we
              do, before I do, before
              I am.

WHEN WE LOVE, OH, OUR EYES

Maybe this —
that we're redeeming
one another —
would we know?

What if
what love is
knows, and we know
it not

and if we did —
could we say
I save you
one to one another
with unguarded eyes?

Surely we would have to veil
our eyes from showing, shield
from seeing you and I

are angels
marrying

— as still we do.

THE GRANDMOTHER dozes. It is a luxury, unfettered by guilt. Drifting, she hears the rumble and lilt of voices: her son and his three-year-old daughter downstairs. They are collaborating on breakfast; their discussion grows spirited, grows calm. Quiet, and probably they're eating. Spoons. She sleeps some more.

Grunts and huffs; the child struggles up onto the bed, wrestles her way down under the covers and, snuggling close to her grandmother's body, sighs.

Perhaps they both sleep, or maybe it's a daydream of sleeping. The child's body radiates heat.

"Nana"

The grandmother decides she can answer without waking – manages only to think her answer, which is brief enough: "Mmm".

"Nana, can I play with your breast?"

The grandmother is awake now, thinks, Now that there is only one, maybe it's more interesting.

"Here, sweetie"

"No, Nana. Can I play with the one in the bathroom?"

WHILE TALKING TO MY FATHER

I smooth the sides of the velvet
box that holds his ashes; I
can see him where he slowly stands
from bending in the garden. There

are beets in his hand. Their leaves
flop over, iron rags. I show him
what I have in my hands.
I show him that my hands
are heavy with the promises
I've made. He says
Have you stopped loving the weight?

He says
I never stopped loving the weight.

WAYS

This is what a woman does
what anybody would
if restless
if possessed of wit:

she dreams
of other ways

and she agrees
with Anna Akhmatova (who borrowed
her grandmother's glorious name
because of its luminous a's)

that if she stepped outside
herself, beheld
herself, she'd know
what envy is; still

she wanders past her
unadorned b's and days
and dreams
of other ways.

DIVESTITURE (MEXICO)

Under the snowy cloth
its shiny forks and spoons
she kicks off her shoes, pretends –
Each shoe subtracts me twenty
years and now I'm twenty-five and this
time without husband and the kids;

she walks. She's glad
to be bereft, glad
to be bare-legs in this green lake, thigh-
deep in water hyacinths and silver glitter-
fish and ooze

this thin mountain light

South down the coast
a brown-skinned brother and his sister
are laying out blue bowls
and cups on a yellow cloth.
Crushed spices breeze intemperate
out the windows of their kitchen. I
am going there.

WE NATURALLY PRAY

There's something in us that burrows
that wants to bow
our head and be blind

like this bee
who tumbles – doesn't he
try to hide in the golden
stamen-forest of this rose?

Somersaults are like that
and making love with eyes closed.

Lucky on the day we die
we'll stumble laden
to the edge that bends
a little under the weight of our leaving
and stagger fervent over the rim.

ABUNDANCE

MEN WHO PLAY TROMBONES
love to play in groups.
Outdoors
at dawn
they stand in canoes
mist rising around them
from black glass
like grass growing.
Lips press
in flat kisses.
They are blow
-brothers, arms
so long
extend-
bend-
slide-
spilling back to woods
the sounds
that came from there.

HOLY WEEK

The city throbs with it –
every flower thrusts forward
a pistil bold as a cock;
lily and amaryllis pour forth pollen
from honey cups, spill it out
like manna into the very
air, sticky with desire.
     A stray
malamute in the studio today
leaped for joy on our legs, pink penis
pointed trustingly to us for home.

Babies everywhere: white knitted blankets
sculpted into cocoons, wee round heads
bobble on Papas' shoulders, babies
in the arms of bigger babies, babies walking, babies
in parades, and one – an infant Jesus
with his holy Ma and Pa on the back of a truck
on Juarez Day.

     Even I
with my gray hair, hear *Hola!*s from young boys.
My friend says, All they want is a nurse
with a purse, but I say

They've got it, the fever,
and I am catching it.

VALENTINE

Beyond the glass, feathered sisters
sport fringed caps,
a small fortune
of over-wintering female cardinals
frisks in the apple hedge
with masked mates – six
darting scarlet exclamation marks.

Here, beneath my breastbone
a thread-thin fissure dashes
the width of my chest
                splits
                spreads, dear
                god, deep boom . . . ice
                breaking up

. . . and this is a lie.

A woman will lie
when her heart is knotted
in ice but remembers it warm
and only wants
to want to love
his long, warm legs again.

TURN

January, and the oak still hangs
from the wrists of his arms ragged
leaves like a few hands of cards
turned bronze, turned down
as if to fold.

In my hands, tatters of old lace
decayed beyond reprieve, dream-
lace of being loved
some other, early
way (and I could turn against
the one who is
my darling one)
and green; how frolicsome
we were, and green

                              as leaves were.
                              Bury the lace now
                              tenderly.

SINGING

He wakes up singing me
a song he composed in his dream.
The words begin I'll always
love you, and the second line

won't scan but says, You mustn't
leave me. So I say, I

woke up with a song, I was
in Mexico and walking
into darkness with new friends
and in that place

the sun would never shine; I can't
explain the joy I feel again

recalling this, and he is puzzled, so
Don't listen to the words, I say, they
don't make sense, but in my dream

they generated joy. He says, I think
my dream's the better one.

MEDUSA (TO PERSEUS)

(1)

Husband, come with me
to the garden. I'm off to uproot
raspberry shoots inched
into the lawn last night.

Tell me your dream – the peaceful
room of sun, beloved women
weaving quietly, the entrance

of another one: her welling
warrior eye, shirtsleeves
up to here, taking up the space
of holy! seven women – eight – a mass
of massasauga rattlers sprung from her scalp

—how you stand and you slay her *(Once and for all!*
you shout), the woman whose voice
you say, is something like mine.

(2)

Once won't do
for all, of course
so let's discuss the snakes.
God knows
how they came to grow from my scalp
but now they're here
there are advantages:

no hats.

I whisk without delay through the checkout
at the Valu-Mart. Joe Campbell and Carl Jung
both speak of them with great respect, "symbolic
of capacity for transformation", that is what they
say – the creature sheds its skin
so it can grow. You cannot
object to that. But it must be said
that if your head's like mine, a nest
of slender, swaying animals with clever eyes
with tongues like neon ruby threads
you'd better be prepared
for big-time loneliness. Out there
they want your hair to sit still. In general
the world defined as western
is not equipped for such arousal, this much
peristaltic pulsing, so much
liveliness.

CWETHAN: A LEGACY
For Greg Curnoe
1936 – 1992

Your bike, like a crumpled mantis
flung by a giant fist . . .
the pickup struck fast
west of Delaware
and you died on the road:
no tender syllables by your bed
no last wishes aloud

But didn't we hear you
fly into the air
(yellow and orange and green, your long legs
shining in black lycra), didn't you
hover over the flooded field
and the Thames unbound as blood?

And didn't we hear you
shout all night
through the dark
and the softly hurtling snow
Go for where the life is!
Go for where the life is!

And didn't we leave our beds
and run from our open doors
into the falling snow
and didn't we shout to the opening sky?
and didn't we answer?

November 15, 1992.

WHAT MAKING LOVE IS FOR

He says he's sure
that God designed all this
so we could be at peace

and I say it's so I can
leap and shine
like a fish
caught   caught.

PRUNING (ISOBEL)

Isobel is on chemo;
two down, three to go.
Today she feels quite well,
her appetite is back
and the lentil soup she makes
smells really good to her
for a change — its cubes
of carrot, little arcs of celery.

For vanity she wears
a paisleyed scarf snug
to her brow, her ears, and tied
behind, a babushka, like the grandmothers
wore in more modest days
when a woman didn't tempt
another woman's man
with the gleam of her hair.
Nor did she

rage out of doors
against the crazed cells invisible
inside her, rage like Isobel
with pruning shears, brutalizing
fruit trees in the yard to stubs
as if they are her puny-hearted
husband, who tended them before he left
her bed to bed another woman, gleaming.

Even before her hair fell out
her heart fell out, got lost
somewhere, and now
she rages it back, chop
by furious chop.

ABUNDANCE: FOR CHARLIE

I am suddenly shy with you today
as if we are the ages of our children,
as if it's you and I
who've given birth to
this borrowed boy and girl,
these children of my son.
Our house,
too happy, sails upon a sea
of ripening grain, fat oats of blue
and silver green
waving   waving.
How radiant the sun
is flung like butter on our walls! Indoors,
the children learn to type,
Placido sings.
              I would keep them

always, if I could,
all these cups running over,
hold them in my throat
my eyes
the hidden room between my legs,
brim full,
              hold them
for you to taste
and drink
when we make love
in winter.

SPRING

We lie awake tonight;
Isobel next door is dying, switches
her bedlight on/off/on

On our south side, in the other
neighbour's backyard pond
spring peepers trill unceasingly
beseechingly, and loud, to mate.

At four a.m., in the dark, a duck
bursts into ecstatic speech – cascades
of liquid duckpurrs; at the last, he
or she utters one self-defining quack, and

the frogs fall silent, seemingly
in awe (it might be envy); we
lie wordless.

THE ENTOMOLOGIST   for Tristan
investigates,
elfin structures pizzicato
skin around his eyes,
his concentration rhythm
slow as endoderm.

Bugs are ectoderm
and are not bugs
but insects (he instructs), are
nervous-system
quiver-many-legged
eating things that wave
their paths through a bantam cosmos
flex minute knees, articulate
atomic jaws.
They are intelligent, small
notched notes in a big song
Pythagoras and poets since
(as I instruct) call music of the spheres,

and he calls **really neat** –
my daughter's omnimorphic son
examining.

UP

Delphinium grows tall this summer, tall
as Julia thirteen, suddenly
loftier than her Mom, shot
up long-legs to the startled
reconnoitering of her brother,
                                          eye-
to-eye with her Dad; Julia
sways slightly in her height, tries
ideas from there; we see
she gleams in the longer view

and now and then
glances down to her knees
where she was before.

CONCH

Two sisters stand as straight as dancers
in their two backyards, two
alike faces of their family
pared down. They hang
familiar wash, pin up
stray hair.
    Gazing away
each notices she waits
for something wonderful.
                              One

suddenly goes indoors and calls her
sister
long-distance after 35 years. She says

Thank
you for sewing my graduation dress.
Thank
you for sending money to Mama.

                              Her
sister
says, Do you remember
Mama calling Papa in at noon
with a conch shell? Where did she get
a conch shell? The other says
O Yes! and Has your hair
turned yet? She says
Sister
when I die
have Elizabeth play the piano.

ALLUREMENT

UPON MY DEATH: INSTRUCTIONS

Let there be woodwinds at the funeral.
Pile my pyre high with old furniture
and let it burn for three days.
Let friends and strangers bring theirs—
chairs, china cupboards they no longer want
—in memory of me
and add them to the fire.
On the fourth day, let the tide pour in on
ashes, iron nails, my numerous teeth
and sweep all out to sea.

Then will the sand be smoothed
as the brows of those who came and went.
Let them forget my name
and let the woodwind players
go home to their strict beds
and in the morning waken
to new contracts
with rich European orchestras.

ALLUREMENT: ON READING JORGE LUIS BORGES' *THIS CRAFT OF VERSE*

I waited hard
today to write the words
of a wine-dark sea, not
that I have ever swum, or
longed to, in that
lurid burgundy, but

I wanted to reach to
Jorge Luis Borges, the syllables
of his name, who tasted blind
Homer's wine-dark words. And I
can feel his love
for the man who chose
to marry the sea and wine. How
it gleams! the brotherhood–
in-art between them, living
and the dead (though Borges now
is dead), the words
alive; I

unseen at the rim
of their shore, come
to be near their rich
affinity.
        How

the wave rushes the pebbles in!
How it rattles them out again!

SEEING JACK CHAMBERS' *LAKE HURON #1* AGAIN

Today all things fly up.
Skin shifts on the backs of my hands
as if you blew there;
something real is realer
than these falls of apples in the grass.
The space between my home and home

where you are falls away. You
dear friend, return. We talk
of ordinary work; I tell you
you left me behind
on empty sand below the yellow cliff.

I slip them off, these
heavy clothes of meat and bone;
women call from porches, but it's too late
for porches. Sky may be too big
and I may be too small, but I

am eager for the lifting-off
and you and I
among the little clouds
fly up, and all the people
that we love fly up.

O – AN ESSAY

O is more difficult
than Oh. Most days
O is so big we cannot
get our arms around
her waist; we add the little handle
h; h tames.

      Truest
human cries are O-
cries: the glossolalia O
of praise, the ululating O
that is a howl of supplication, O O O
the endless, unaccented O of grief.

Braided in them all
is Awe, the O before her name
is spoken, she who interweaves
as swallows interleaf each other, looping
before dark above the park; she

rivers our cells with root
intentions, reaves us, loosens
the weave of us, leaves
us changed
                (angels of all ages
                billow in; before
                we were sizes 12 and 44, now
                we are huge and still
                expanding…) O

is only a shape on a page for this!

ALLUREMENT (STRAYCHILD)

An hour ago I spooned
strained carrots into her tiny mouth
with a silver coffee spoon   Now
the baby is lost in the grass

I need to say
she cannot sit up alone
nor did she suckle strong   My nipple
fell from her wet mouth   I said
to the watchers   The baby's

full of carrots   but I lied
about that   She was weak
ready to leave   I believe

she sank into grass
grown thick at the verge of the dark
that stands patient behind us always
murmuring, however we turn

SOUTHERN TREES

This didn't have a name
when I was young, but I breathed
it in and thus was partly made
of the patient longing of my father, yearning
years and years for boyhood walnuts
up and down Mount Vernon Street

and I was partly made
of James William's soul's
last turning home, he slowly
bleeding into the soft grass
of Chancellorsville, dreaming
the rough black arms of locust trees
around the house and either side
the bright clay trace down to the Baltimore Pike.

                Homesickness
is a happiness returned; I know
a spell of sand whose palms
make exclamations on the sky; a dolphin
swam there, who followed
me and talked beside me walking
long and long St. Simon's Island's beach
I nearly had forgot; often

I've thought my home
is someplace southern with trees, lavish
with fruit that
for a moment
I have just forgot.

Photo: W.A. Thompson

Their Beneficence

My thanks to these generous readers: Maxine Kumin, Charles Mackenzie, and Thelma Rosner; to Stan Dragland, Cornelia Hoogland, Ann Lindsay, and Joanne Page.

My deep gratitude to Molly Peacock. You know your worth.

My ardent appreciation for her unfailing support, to Marnie Parsons, my editor.

Viva! to the Banff Centre for the Arts and the 1997 Writing Studio, which gave me five weeks in a place of unforgettable camaraderie and beauty, and the inspiration of Tim Lilburn and Don McKay.

Words in Tim Lilburn's essay, "Two Books About Love" (*The Fiddlehead*, Spring, 1999) resonated their way into "Could We Know".

Sandra DeSalvo, for reproducing the manuscript, and Lise Downe, for permission to reproduce your painting, "First Blush", thanks, thanks.

Thank you, Maureen Harris, for shepherding these pages into a book.

To John Tamblyn, for heroism in translating Lise's painting onto the cover, a gold medal.

Acknowledgements

These poems first appeared in *Canadian Forum*: "Men Who Play Trombones", "What Making Love Is For", "Seeing Jack Chambers' *Lake Huron #1* Again", and "Pruning (Isobel)."

"Abundance: For Charlie" first appeared in *The Fiddlehead*, as did "Upon My Death: Instructions". The latter poem was selected for *Fiddlehead Gold: Fifty Years of The Fiddlehead Magazine Anthology*.

"Holy Week" was published in *Prairie Fire*.

My thanks to these editors and publishers.

About the artist

Lise Downe painted for many years and is the author of three books of poetry, most recently *Disturbances of Progress* (Coach House Books, 2002). Originally from London, Ontario, she resides in Toronto where she continues to write and make jewellery.

Susan Downe is a retired psychotherapist, a gardener, a wife, daughter, mother, and grandmother, who has made the reading and writing of poems a central part of her days since 1991.

Her praise-poem, "Between This ... And This", was published by Spanish Onion Press in 1998.

She continues work on a fiction/ memoir project, of her mother's girlhood, in Texas County, Missouri.